Ride the Blue Roan

Ride the Blue Roan

John Weier

TURNSTONE PRESS

Copyright © 1988 John Weier

Published with the assistance of the Manitoba Arts Council and the Canada Council.

Turnstone Press
607-100 Arthur Street
Winnipeg, Manitoba
R3B 1H3 Canada

This book was printed by Hignell Printing Limited for Turnstone Press.

Printed and bound in Canada

Cover design: Roger Lusty

The author gratefully acknowledges a writers' "B" grant from the Manitoba Arts Council.

Some of these poems have appeared, in this or some other form, in *Anerca, edges, Mennonite Mirror, Prairie Fire, Prairie Journal of Canadian Literature* and *Rainbow Papers*.

Canadian Cataloguing in Publication Data

Weier, John, 1949-

   Ride the blue roan

   Poems.
   ISBN 0-88801-131-8

I. Title.

PS8595.E418R5 1988   C811'.54   C88-098106-7
PR9199.3.W44R5 1988

for Anna and Jonathan

Light hovers
at the foot of a Dutch bridge.
It is morning.
No one comes.
                George Amabile

And Jacob was left alone; and there wrestled
a man with him, until the breaking of the day.
                Genesis 32:24

I only buy used mirrors now. I like to see
other faces when I look at myself.
                Robert Kroetsch

Contents

DREAMS AND HORSES

inheritance   2
father the rain and i   3
mother dreams   4
who is this woman   6
childhood and russia   7
woman talk   9
matchmaker   11
hitching post   12
buddha and the boat   13
east wind   14
we have always been lonely   15
in terms of an empty chair   16
blue cross   17
four paintings   18
haiku of gravity   19
horse sense   20
jed   21
coal black   22
simply wolf willow   23

FOOTNOTES TO DALE   25

TRAIN JOURNALS   65

Dreams and Horses

inheritance

out driving this morning, i saw swallows. tanned bellies, dark back and wings shining in the sun. pocket nests perched against concrete.

years ago, on the russian steppes, swallows lived in grandfather's barn. my father, still a boy, waited for them in spring. the first swallow meant he could leave his shoes behind for summer, let his toes wander in the dust. he watched them gather mud to build their nests. saw the hungry little mouths, awkward wingbeat turn to adult flight. then suddenly, missed them, gone in fall.

our old barn in niagara had plenty of openings big enough for nesting swallows to enter. but when we built the new one, doors had to be left open all spring and summer. if the season was dry i had to carry water, make mud for their nests.

this morning, as we cross the misericordia bridge, they still hover near their young, slide through air filled with chattering song. my son and daughter wonder what they're called.

father the rain and i

midday
a dark sky
it is raining
large drops parachute to earth
the wind has stopped
i stand at the open door of the barn
my father beside me
we have no time no
need for work now
only the rain
watching the rain
watching it fall
large drops
to the earth
no wind
no thought
of danger to the crops
those times have fled
hold no meaning
only the rain my father and i
the rain smell the air
only watching the pleasure of the rain
father and i
in our cocoon
he stands beside me
the air around us silk and warm
rain touches the earth

mother dreams

    1

she is dead and in her coffin
he is standing there
looking
angry
for the first time

    2

her standing
over his bed   wanting
to ease his suffering   he
watches his right hand
strike
into being
against her face

    3

he rushes from the house
it is burning
his mother
waits at the door
angry   he throws
curses in her face
and steps into the darkness

4

the womb is
an empty cavern
ribs above   below
a reddish twilight
he stands alone
has
no connection

5

finds himself
pushed
into the world
caught
by sterile hands   then
reaching for a breast   he's
pushed again

6

she is dead and in her coffin
he is standing there
looking   he is
angry
for the first time

who is this woman

there is a woman who hangs in my dreams wrists
knotted above her head she has dark hair skin wears a
long skirt her breasts are swollen bleeding green pus
cheek resting against her shoulder she mumbles
words something about forsaken the sky is black
people are watching there is a woman who hangs in
my dreams i wonder who will save her

childhood and russia

1

his mother's russia
was a terrible place
full of things not
to be remembered
       she never spoke of it

her mother dying when she was two. an ordinary
illness. father when she was four, some say a broken
heart. the children went to live with their
grandparents. but some things aren't easily left
behind. grandfather died before she turned six. he
was old.

i wonder if anybody warned her   she
may not have believed it anyway
it wasn't
believable

during the revolution, now living in the home of her
aunt, his mother watched from a wheat field at night
as her home and village burnt to the ground. in 1926,
the family boarded a ship. they were going to canada.
the aunt's children were buried at sea. his mother, the
stepchild, survived.

canada was the land of hope. still, her first child died
before it was two. after that she spoke often of
heaven, things would be better in heaven.

is there life
after death
so much death

2

his father, at seventy-six, wakes every morning in ontario. eats his breakfast. then walks from one end of the village in russia to the other. past the janzens, the wiebes, the driedgers. sits on his father's lap, tugging at his moustache. rides vangka down the street for the first time, sliding into the mud, just as the big horse turns up the lane. watches the peasants singing and dancing round the fire, after the threshing is done on his father's farm. goes off to school with his friends nick and isbrandt. they are laughing.

those were the best
years of his life

3

what a
beautiful
tragedy

woman talk

1

a man sits at a table in the cafeteria   obviously
waiting   a woman appears   walking slowly   she
is carrying coffee   their eyes meet   faces soften
no voices   only eyes and faces   smiles   finally
he sips his juice   they talk   laugh together   he
has brought hand written pages   poems   she
reads   pauses   smiles her reply   reads   he
looks at the rings on her finger   they talk
suddenly   she turns to her watch   their eyes shift
voices break   faces fall   she has to go
someone is waiting

2

the woman smiles an invitation   her thighs are the
whitest he has ever imagined   he has watched them
hiding under her dress   now turns to touch them
soft and trembling to the breath of his caress   lips
erase the final line of hesitation   his mouth
reaching to taste her desire   man's tongue
woman's body   together they can speak forgotten
words   skin on skin a bath in living water

3

said she needed some space   time to think   clear
her head   just a few days to herself   he
understood   felt that way himself sometimes   it
was no problem   until this morning   sunday
the waiting is becoming unbearable   why hasn't
she called   what did she mean about space   and
that car parked on the street in front of her house
he won't call her   is reluctant to leave the
apartment   what if she calls and he's not in
the telephone stares at him in silence   he wonders
if it's out of order

matchmaker
(for bob)

yesterday, over a drink, you asked if i'd ever looked
back and wondered what i'd seen in her

i
couldn't think
didn't answer

when we were young we'd sometimes snicker and
say, put a bag over it

she wasn't pretty
her dress
   smelled old and stale

but
   i had just flown in
      alone
   she   it turns out
      was dying

beneath
   the clothes features skin
      we were a perfect match
   bodies clinging to each other
      shining in the night

hitching post
(for jan)

got into yorkton early sunday afternoon   the others
weren't arriving until later so i decided to go for a
walk   stretch my legs after the trip from regina

thought i saw you drive by   it seemed unlikely   i
knew you hadn't been here since childhood   still
the impression was so strong

and later   walking up and down broadway the sun
warm on my skin   i felt you beside me   showed
you a tie i liked   a car i might someday own   you
laughed   once i almost caught your reflection as we
admired a saddle in the window of the hitching post

yours

buddha and the boat

a few minutes ago i was sitting in my back yard. now i am here beside this lake. i am on the beach. the waves are large, washing against the shore. it is a good feeling, the waves and i, nothing else, only the waves rising and washing within me.

i see a boat. a strange boat, small and wide. a man stands in it, left hand on the mast. the waves are loud, i cannot hear him, but he beckons sharply. i am to join him.

the man is peter. he and i standing in a boat, sailing in a storm that has been raging for centuries. peter, still standing hand on the mast, face into the wind. the storm is fierce. perhaps i am frightened. i wonder if i will hear a voice and the water will suddenly be still.

is it really peter? i might be wrong. it could be moses whose hand is on the mast. no one is steering. why am i here? why has he taken me? he seems to have no regard for my safety, doesn't seem to care if i am frightened. does he know i am here? i finally ask where we are going. he says we are sailing. the storm is too loud, he hasn't heard clearly. why are we sailing? the wind shrieks. he says yes. he must have taken me out here for a reason. there is something he wishes to show me. i ask if he has a message for me.

the waves are large and it is raining. the storm is fierce. his left hand is firm on the mast. face into the wind. we are sailing.

east wind

buddhabuddhabuddhabuddhabuddhab
uddhabuddhabuddhabuddhabuddhabu
ddhabuddhabuddhabuddhabuddhabud
dhabuddhabuddhabuddhabuddhabudd
habuddhabuddhabuddhabuddhabuddh
abuddhabuddhabuddhabuddhabuddha
buddhabuddhabuddhabuddhabuddhab
uddhabuddhabuddhabuddhabuddhabu
ddhabuddhabuddhabuddhabuddhabud
dhabuddhabuddhabuddhabuddhabudd
habuddhabuddhabuddhabuddhabuddh
abuddhabuddhabuddhabuddhabuddha
buddhabuddhabuddhabuddhabuddhab
uddhabuddhabuddhabuddhabuddhabu
ddhabuddhabuddhabuddhabuddhabud
dhabuddhabuddhabuddhabuddhabudd
habuddhabuddhabuddhabuddhabuddh
abuddhabuddhabuddhabuddhabuddha

we have always been lonely

1.

several years ago, on christmas day, friends of mine called at seven in the evening. they had spent the day with their children and grandchildren. now, suddenly, everyone was gone. they were lonely. would i be interested in coming over?

2.

on holiday in tel aviv, a violinmaker once wrote to tell me about all the things he was doing. *otherwise,* he ended, *this far from my tools i am feeling very lonely, i think you must know what i mean.*

3.

a friend once told me that he had never been as lonely as when he was still married.

4.

in a remote hut somewhere in tibet, a man has chosen to live in seclusion. he is a lama, and spends his time in meditation. supplies are left at his door on a monthly basis. he has seen no one for three years. sometimes he thinks he should be lonely.

in terms of an empty chair

1.

tonight, i am lonely. i am no longer sure it is for you. it is for everyone and no one, everything and nothing. it simply is.

2.

a teacher of mine thinks that loneliness can best be described in terms of an empty chair. it's a good idea, but somehow tonight i can't think of a chair large or strong enough.

3.

in a poem about a forest and lake, a loon and the stars, i once heard a poet speak the words, *we have always been lonely.* though neither he nor i have ever found the line again, i am sure it is the greatest he has ever written.

blue cross

i hadn't been feeling very good. of course, it didn't help that i was in my mid thirties, recently separated, and out of a job. a friend of mine, sensing my unhappiness, suggested i go see her doctor.

i had heard about him on the news a few years ago. he practised holistic medicine. authorities, not pleased with his unconventional ideas, had suspended his medical license.

i went to see him. maybe i wasn't eating the right kind of food, or maybe i had some unusual allergy. i was hoping he might have an easy cure for my condition.

he asked a lot of questions. what i ate, how often i exercised, why my wife and i had separated. then, he held onto one outstretched arm while i clutched an assortment of marked containers with the hand of the other. it seemed a little strange.

when i was finally ready to leave, he told me that what i really needed was god. but, in the meantime, if i put a tablespoon of this certain powder in my orange juice every morning, it would leave my bowels cleaner than they'd ever been.

it was good advice.

four paintings

he is in an artist's studio. in the corner an easel. canvases fastened to the walls. on a table, a shoe box half full of oil sticks, scattered pieces of charcoal, tubes of acrylic paint, a jar of turpentine, some brushes.

he has decided to become a painter. in this life he will do four paintings.

one is of a large brilliant ball of white light. the light is in motion, spinning. as he watches, it envelops him. his body feels quiet, but fresh.

the second is about colour. bursts of orange, red, green, yellow, blue. here and there a streak of black. it is done with a sense of freedom and joy.

another, looks like trees and northern lights. lines of bright green, vertical, horizontal, dancing, growing thick and thin. behind the movement of green, empty.

the centre of the last, a shining core of blue. the colour fading past the edges of the canvas, the same blue but lighter. or darker. possibly both.

haiku of gravity

    1

today i reach
for a fly ball
my feet too old to leave the ground

    2

the wild sound of geese
in an ancient sky
my feet have grown roots

horse sense

this is the winter i dream of horses

a hundred belgians lying dead in a field of
melting snow   legs stuck sideways in the air
like the toy horses i played with as a child

arabians running in a paddock   mane and tail
feathered against the wind   heads high   eyes
turned back to watch me   they are runaways
always running yet always near enough to see
me

i dream of wrecks   quarter horses wrestling
with wagons trucks   one dying under an oldsmobile
eyes still fastened to my face

this is a show they're putting on for me   they
taunt me and sneer at my reaction

the team of clydesdales i am driving through
the heavy snow is pulling hard   i am getting
tired   cannot hold them much longer   and they
are running   running   farther and farther

and i am left behind   growing old

a child of two wakes in the night shouting *horses
horses* as a herd of wild ones rages through his
bedroom

jed

ahead of us jed rides the blue roan   loose in the
saddle body moves with his horse   his hand reaches
up to grab his hat   holds it while twisting to pull a
sweater over his head with the other   god knows
what he's done with the reins   the sweater comes
on but his head can't find the hole   he's caught
there while the roan picks its way across the shale
finally the head appears   and jed's pudgy six year
old hand reaches back for the sandwich packed in his
saddlebag

coal black

just never thought to check

we were pulling one of those long gooseneck cattle
trailers   the road was bumpy but we were
managing a steady fifty

suddenly   we felt the truck lurch as though it had
lost weight   and there she was   horrible   in my
rear-view mirror   legs body neck thrashing over
and over   and sliding   and coming to a quiet heap
on the road   brakes jammed   tires screaming   i
felt sick   couldn't wait for reverse   out of the
truck and running   the back gate open   god
and her such a beautiful mare   struggling to get up
long black legs back left twisting at the hock all
bloodied right shoulder flesh scraped to the bone
standing there and i was sick her still standing there
hot blood thoroughbred

then finally crumbling   and gone

simply wolf willow
(for carp)

spent the last few days in the cypress hills. as we drive you count antelope, deer, talk of giant brown trout. the sky is blue. hills fall and rise, they have never touched a plough. we see cattle, large herds of herefords, horses, cowboys, hats and boots.

this land grows from a young boy's dreams, a home where the buffalo roam

finally, we dip into the valley and eastend. we need gas. at the service station we pull up beside the pumps and a yellow school bus.

i ask a short burly man in blue jean and red lumberjack if he knows where sharon lives. i'm sure he hasn't even heard of her. he says he does, but adds that it'll be impossible to get out there today because of last night's rain. i thank him and go pay for the gas.

when i return, he's waiting. wants to know if i've read her latest book. it's only been in print four weeks. i tell him i have. his oh is low and falling. he's disappointed, thought he might have had something on this tall dark stranger. as though living here isn't enough.

Footnotes to Dale

8/8/86

i'm sorry i was so angry at you this morning, it's not easy always having you around.

i get along with people best when i'm alone

12/8/86

when he was four, we played baseball every day. that plastic bat and ball. he was always the batter.

i wonder how he survived that time. my anger, impatience. somehow our game was worth nothing to me.

four years later it's easier. he's grown up, can catch and throw

and he's forgiven. this morning in the car, i don't know whether to laugh or cry. he is quiet for a long time, looks up at me and says, *you know dad, i was born for baseball.* quiet again, then, *babe ruth and i are sort of the same, you know.*

16/8/86

this morning on the bus, a woman is telling a friend about the new pony she bought. her boyfriend drives a colt, bought it after his mustang broke down

makes you wonder what they'll be driving next. maybe a horsetrailer.

i have to restrain myself, keep from leaning across the aisle to tell them about the liver chestnut i ride every sunday morning.

20/8/86

the moon isn't full.

environment canada tells me that the barometric pressure is not plunging desperately, but is steady at 101 kilopascals.

then, on cbc, i hear that sometimes collapsing stars cause huge gravitational waves, like the shaking of a universal blanket.

i'm relieved, i was beginning to think it was me.

29/8/86

i'm glad you decided to go away for your holidays. the phone has finally stopped ringing. i have time to read and write. the cat is curled up on the couch, i can hear it purring from here. i am sleeping well

30/8/86

when will you be back?

31/8/86

spent the day with my kids. we went grocery shopping. bought, among other things, a jar of welch's grape juice. they were determined to be helpful. so there we were, in the lobby of my apartment block with grape juice running from the bottom of one of the bags. there's something about jars and concrete floors

i was furious.

but now, looking back, i wish i could tell them i love them

1/9/86

the kids and i drive to winkler to visit friends.

(i don't know how to say it, i'm sure the words will make it false)

it is morning
the sky vast blue
patches of trees, some bold green, others passing to
    colour
the grain is golden
the fallow brown
versatile, red and yellow, whispers goodnight to the
    soil
a herd of red cows, a fall-born calf still wet, an
    anxious mother

the earth too bright for words

2/9/86

anna's first day of school.

thirty one years ago the same thing happened to me.

johnny and carol
sitting in a tree
k i s s i n g

carol, wherever you are, do you know that i still dream about you? last night we were at the zoo, the tigers got out of their cage and chased us.

did you survive

16/9/86

sitting under a tree in the desert, i watch a long string of camels pass by. hundreds of camels, striped and spotted, camels blue and yellow, some filled with rage, others fear or laughter. camel after camel ambling by in that peculiar camel way. the whole string finally floating off into the spirit sand.

18/9/86

tonight, ondaatje reading *secular love*. songs of warmth, of thighs and tenderness and touch. i have loved desperately too. for now, my heart is cold.

26/9/86

the boy is lying in bed, unable to sleep. he is thinking about his father. remembering when his father was still at home to greet him after a day at school. the after supper baseball games when he was five. his father's terrier. he wonders about his father's life. what does he do with all his time alone? does he wonder what the boy thinks about as he waits for sleep to come?

27/9/86

she is twenty-seven and surprised. didn't think she'd like it.

says it tastes salty.

27/9/86

it is ten p.m. we are driving down a well lit street in st. paul, minnesota. she begins to unbutton the blouse she is wearing. i notice she has already taken off her bra. she seems a little shy, reluctant, slouches in her seat. but as she removes her skirt, insists that this is something she has to do.

in downtown st. paul, with a naked woman beside me, i am worried she'll catch cold. who might see.

28/9/86

brandon, minnesota, a small town.

we have lunch at the blue gill cafe. four bass and a mallard on the north wall. in the corner, three elderly women talk about who was in church this morning. a young couple gets up to leave. he has a farm face, wears cowboy boots. outside our window, he opens the car door, she gets in from his side. they sit close together. a tall heavy-set man comes in, announces that he has come to watch the football game. there is a tv at the back. the vikings are winning. someone across the room asks whether his isn't working yet.

recognition is heavily striped with sorrow. i crawl under tables looking for something i'm sure i've lost

3/10/86

last night
your best friend
breathless, tongue around inside my ear

dreaming
and you lying not an arm's length away

i know, i really am shameless
(but please, don't forget to tell her she
was wonderful).

4/10/86

tonight, readings by george faludy, hungarian poet.
survivor of war, prison, torture, and finally, freedom.
faludy with his einstein face and hair, a story in life
and poem. small man, big enough to grasp the horrors
of a century. frail, yet strong enough to stand and
smile. at midnight, when he stops speaking, there is
nothing left to say.

8/10/86

hotel saskatchewan, regina

dear laura

six months ago, we were here together. sunday morning, a cloudless sky, the church bells, remembering hymns as only lost believers can.

was that the last time i kissed you?

12/10/86

in russia when father was young, he was told to prepare for the trip to canada. the voyage, by sea, would be long and difficult, hard on a boy's stomach. there was a swing hanging from the willow tree. the best thing he could do, they said, was to spend as much time swinging as possible. he wasn't seasick once.

13/10/86

even as he jumps, i know what will happen

it's too rushed. he slides off balance, flips forward, my stomach jumps, chest screaming. then, he is in the sand. head down, twisted. i am afraid.

in a second he's up. mouth wide, full of dirt, staring. when he cries i can hardly bear it.

eight years old, he is the only son i have.

21/10/86

business in banff. i've planned to stay a few extra days. it should be a good place to work on my book of poems.

now i'm here. mountains all around. huge rocks waiting to be written. and i am wordless

30/10/86

tonight again. just as i am sliding into sleep, mother approaches the bed. it is dark, my eyes are closed, still, i can see her. i know why she has come. know, in some dark and hidden place, the message that she carries. know that, once more, i will startle out of sleep and she will be gone.

30/10/86

this morning's flight, winnipeg to edmonton, reminds me of an old love affair.

all ups and downs, white knuckles, gasping breath, a knotted stomach. when will the falling end? a stopover of calm in regina, then turbulence again.

i hope this
ends better

2/11/86

mayfield inn

maybe i could stay here forever.
outside, edmonton turns to winter. it is cold, grey, windy.

my room is warm. i have a book of poetry, advice from a friend. i have paper and a pen

5/11/86

in the library lounge of the calgary centre inn with trevor. we are talking about poetry and the east. suddenly, an old memory slips off my tongue.

in 1976, all of north america was obsessed with speed-reading. instant knowledge, know everything in thirty minutes or less. but in the mahatma ghandi library at the university of delhi, inscribed on the wall, i read the words of a single-minded man. *only learn to read slowly, and all the other virtues will follow.*

11/11/86

i don't understand your reaction to airports. i can't even think the word without you getting angry.

15/11/86

the brownstone, toronto.
can't sleep, someone next door is snoring.

back in my college days, i had a room-mate from
china. a nice fellow, middle aged, friendly. but we did
have problems.

one, he snored terribly. and two, he had a black belt
in judo. it was impossible to sleep. i finally resorted
to shaking his bed, hoping that he would wake up
enough to turn over. i didn't want to shake too hard. i
wasn't sure that an asian with all the right moves
would have much patience with my mennonite, kid
from the farm, naivete. nothing helped.

16/11/86

i know all the logic, the stats, know the huge risk of
highway travel. but at 33,000 feet, toronto to
winnipeg, i lose all touch with reason. here, this far
above the earth, i think only of buckled landing gear,
of tiny cessnas nudging through cloud to kiss our 727,
of air traffic controllers dreaming the thighs of last
night's lovers.

6/12/86

called june, she said she'd really believed i'd never think of her again.

9/12/86

suddenly, childhood and russia. a poem i've been writing for over half a century.

10/12/86

today, the first review of *after the revolution*. with christmas greetings from a friend

a poet's not a poet
till he writes a poem that rhymes
even though he keeps on writing
until the end of time

at least i know he's read it.

(he hasn't included any punctuation in his poem. has he forgotten, or was it intentional?)

14/12/86

i once had a friend who played the mandolin. he died too young. maybe wasn't strong enough for being human, i don't know. this afternoon i catch him hiding behind a chair in my living room, he's spying on me. likes to see how things are developing

17/12/86

so this time it's you talking about airports. running off to join your family in palm springs. at least i've never left at christmas. don't get me wrong, i'm not feeling sorry for myself. i've been alone before.

18/12/86

after breakfast, you smile at me and say, *three times a day keeps the doctor away.*

i'm not sure i understand, perhaps you could teach me

21/12/86

yes, i have a christmas tree. it keeps falling over

22/12/86

i was pulling on my cowboy boots. you were sitting on the couch opposite, and said something about, what's the point, is it really worth it.

old questions. still, things hadn't been easy for you, i didn't know what to say. feeling my foot slide into an old habit, i suddenly knew it was.

now, you're half a continent away, and i'm not so sure.

25/12/86

a) a game of solitaire

b) won at solitaire

c) lost at solitaire

d) all of the above

6/1/87

this morning walking to the university of manitoba, i'm scared to smile at the old man i pass on the sidewalk. afraid to feel the bite of cold on my skin. later at work, hot and anxious about possible failure

i have chosen fear as today's companion.

7/1/87

i was studying my lunch, it was liver, and decided i'd finally had enough. for three years i'd been punishing myself. three years, or was it thirty-three, with guilt and torture and shame. beginning today, after this sandwich, i will devote my life to pleasure. pleasure, and you, and you and pleasure, and me and you and pleasure

9/1/87

three years since i stopped making instruments, gave up the knife and gouge and plane.

now suddenly, violins fall from the woodwork, guitars dance in my dreams. this morning a 'cello giving birth in the laundry room

10/1/87

this morning lying in your arms, my head against your breast, i couldn't keep from crying.

no real reason.

11/1/87

my father used to keep a bag of peanuts on the hot air-duct in our basement when i was a child. they were his. still, he always looked a little awkward when we found him there with his hand in the bag, as though he wished he hadn't been caught.

he and i have hardly spoken since mother died, and i gave up my marriage.

did you know? the peanut is a brazilian herb, a member of the pea family. it has yellow flowers.

13/1/87

margaret laurence memorial, st. john's college chapel.

what are we doing in this place? when we meet, we meet for beer or scotch, never in a chapel. here, the ceilings are high. there is a natural light. the drone of brass and pipe swirls us into open space, we could fall forever. our bodies tremble. we sing songs, whisper prayers we no longer believe in. we all turn christian in the end

20/1/87

james called. he's going to an eye doctor. thinks his vision is clouding over. he says that everything he sees lacks the clarity and brilliance it had when he was younger. he is intent on reversing the process.

22/1/87

suitcases by aganetha dyck, opening at the ukrainian cultural centre.

wonderful show, and i don't like that kind of art. "recycled." when i left i was thinking of immigrants and canada and mennonite weddings.

22/1/87

tonight in the pocket of someone else's parka

> a crumpled letter from a lawyer, re.
>   the estate of
> a bill from christmas presents 1983
> newsletter from a real estate agency
> matchbook from a pub in new orleans, eleven
>   years ago

now those are pockets worth picking.

i, on the other hand, make sure everything moves from pocket to garbage at the end of every day.

22/1/87

two friends from years ago playing at the st. james legion. an older woman gets up to dance. she looks beaten. shoulders and even her face seem to slump. suddenly, as the music changes time, her body jumps and she is sixteen again.

24/1/87

you've come in from minus 30, late afternoon winnipeg. this, that, and a gallon of white latex you thought you'd closed, balance at chest level. you trip on a flake of snow, and suddenly there's paint all up and down the front of your parka, new mukluks, and a puddle on the carpet. all i can do is laugh and tell you how great you look in white.

i'm so relieved you weren't listening.

25/1/87

somehow, i haven't been able to look you in the face lately. i don't know what's wrong. this morning while you were still sleeping, i pulled a pillowcase over my head. did you notice?

28/1/87

letter from a sister in south america.

p.s. we got your book

thank god she didn't read it.

1/2/87

i think february must be the month of wishes. in february i wish. i wish that twenty years from now my children will have their children. by then i may have spent my restless blood. then i may be the kind of grandfather that children read about at bedtime.

10/2/87

reading blaise/mukerjee's *days and nights in calcutta*.

ten years ago i was there. can still remember the heat, the smell, the music of taxi horns and the cah of crows at 6 o'clock in the morning.

11/2/87

my flight leaves twenty minutes late. as the plane gathers speed, i notice a red fox just off the runway. his plumed tail is heavy against the snow. i'm glad he waited.

when we land in saskatoon he has changed gender and species, now a white-tailed deer.

11/2/87

saskatoon

frank's wife, beth, died the year i was born. since then, he tells me, he's lived at the bessborough hotel. i look surprised, it seems a lifetime to me. but frank says he may be a little older than he looks. back in the fifties a lot of people in the bessborough were permanent residents, now he's the only one left. in 1970 frank visited a nursing home, thought he might move in. decided it wasn't for someone healthy like him. he tells me he can still touch the floor without bending his knees, he feels quite limber. his arms move in sweeping circles to prove it. at 93, frank thinks he's still a little too young for nursing homes.

12/2/87

tell patrick i have met the dalai lama. i was disappointed at first. he is small, has a shy manner, quick smile. he seems quite normal, only slightly older than i. how can anyone so young have anything to teach me.

but then i saw his eyes. they are clear, and as deep as a glacial lake. the moment they touched mine, i fell into them and drowned.

17/2/87

at the winnipeg international airport i see two men wearing handcuffs and leg irons. they are moving from prison to prison. their stride is short, awkward, i think of hobbled horses. one smokes a two-handed cigarette. a door opens, there is a gust of winter air. in that moment, i can smell my freedom, and their humiliation.

17/2/87

the moment of terror. i arrive at the calgary airport. here, there are no old habits, haunts to wrap my spirit in. streets, faces are strange. the room i have taken is the wrong smell, colour. like a child i chant my most familiar mantra, waiting for someone to come.

1/3/87

stopped for egg rolls in a chinese restaurant in carman, manitoba. you and i were the only ones there. a fortune cookie spoke of my longing to see the great pyramids of egypt.

driving home we were lonely.

17/3/87

i can only write in airports and strange hotels.

22/3/87

and now you're going away for easter. i made a hell of a fuss though didn't i? first christmas, now easter! i couldn't let you know how glad i really was. i write better poems when you're away.

26/3/87

spring. one neighbour complains because it's still so cold. the other because it's getting muddy. the bus driver growls at me. and i can tell from the curl of your lips that you've been drinking grapefruit juice again.

29/3/87

i round a corner. there are deer grazing along highway 12. a head comes up, two, three, tails, and they're running. off to find another quiet spot, spring grass, before the coming of the car, this road. what would they write in a journal

in vassar, i stop at a little store for directions. i am noticed, a stranger. the woman at the counter is reading lewis carroll, her name is alice. i can never quite believe that people live this far from home, the city.

160 acres of forest for sale. deer in your garden, bear in your dreams, moose stopping by to say hello. 160 acres of forest. i try to walk quietly, not too sure what might lurk behind the next tree. could i transplant

31/3/87

you called, said you were afraid your father was going to die. why are you worried, he probably will. it's something we carry in our pockets.

once, when jonathan was five, we were out for a drive. he pointed out the window at a cemetery and asked what it was. i explained to him that it was where you buried people after they died. he looked relieved, said he was glad they had such places. it's not something you laugh at every day, but his words caught me by surprise. he thought it wouldn't look nice if dead people were lying around in ditches, don't you think?

4/4/87

he says it in a quiet voice, he's born again. i'm surprised, i'll admit. and he's right, i've never had much use for that kind of thing. still, i know where he's been, know what's run in his veins. and just for once, it's a relief to think he might be safe for awhile.

6/4/87

i don't think i ever saw my mother angry. maybe she didn't dare, too many things had gone wrong already. maybe she saved it all. now, she strides through my dreams in black robes, fists clenched, arms waving.

6/4/87

still all these angry words about my mother. sometimes i wonder if i'm seeing her at all.

7/4/87

remembering a year ago, in a van full of books. it was spring, melting snow, fields in water, ditches rushing off to somewhere. birds, ducks, geese all around. david and i, tired, trading angry words about varieties. (anyone could see they were mallards.) it took four weeks to drive saskatchewan.

today, sitting in an office, we agree it was hardly enough.

7/4/87

daylight saving time again. coming home after work, sun still high in the sky. i am restless, don't feel right, something inside. thinking of my youth, of summer and work, summer on the farm and work, and work and the farm, and nothing but work from sun-up to sundown, and always the feeling of still more to do, and waiting for winter when it's cold and dark, and there's nothing you can do about it now but let it snow, and let the work drift, and you can lie down on the couch with a book, and know that nothing else matters.

10/4/87

after the movie the car takes us down higgins past the old c.p. station. if dad was here, he'd tell us that this was where he last saw his father. that was in 1943 when grandfather moved to ontario. we drive past acklands where dad used to buy supplies for blacksmithing. up streets, across bridges, and past the st. boniface hospital where my children were born.

11/4/87

you say you hate men, then why are your skirts getting shorter? maybe there's no connection.

13/4/87

we need to talk about this.

if it is true as you say, that i treat you like a child, then i suppose you must also treat me like your father. this is getting complicated. i wish you would just grow up. but failing that, do you think we could meet. maybe somewhere in the middle

17/4/87

when i wake this morning, there is blood on my hands. blood on a towel in the bathroom. i don't know where it comes from, what i have done. if anything. i rehearse my dreams, no clues, they have nothing to do with me.

18/4/87

didn't sleep well. the blood still on my mind.

19/4/87

those things i said on monday. have you forgiven me? can you ever forgive me? will you speak to me again

20/4/87

do i have to say it again? yes, i am guilty. i thought the tie i was wearing was green.

25/4/87

i can see it clearly now. there is another man. and all this time i believed you when you said he was your father.

21/5/87

winnipeg to regina, 5:30 a.m.

rain, rain, rain falling. rain against my windshield. and i am thinking of my bedroom thirty years ago, the sound of the rain drumming on the roof not four feet above my head, the comfort of that song, the smiling soft sleep of a child.

21/5/87

we are explorers, you and i, navigating the prairie. crossing the waters of the red river, the assiniboine, la salle, whitemud, souris, cypress, seine. rat creek, squirrel creek, gopher. each finger of water a promise on the other side. the highway pulls us on

21/5/87

rain, rain. thinking of my father and the farm. dad, where are you? we left early this morning hoping to catch you.

23/5/87

dropped in to see peter. we had an argument. he thinks i should be more political. i told him i'd voted twice for the liberals, twice for the conservatives, and twice for the ndp. what more did he want?

he handed me a slice of grapefruit and said no more.

26/5/87

at a baseball clinic.

i've just thrown the ball. my daughter, intent on something across the diamond, has crept too close to the baseline. the throw is bad, pulls far to the left, and suddenly the world stops. there are hours of silence as the ball, in slow motion, arches toward her. the ball twisting and sliding, and i can't even find the time to pray. i am hot and frozen as it sails by just to the side of her curly hair

and finally i can breathe again.

29/5/87

he is angry with me, and i'm not even sure he knows. he has no idea how hard i try to please him.

30/5/87

today, the second time in a week i got out of the tub to smell my father. that clean saturday evening smell of thirty years ago.

5/6/87

you say you'd like to get married. please trust me, it's not a good idea. when i've done something that's meant to be forever, it never seems to last very long.

10/6/87

lena and i on a sunday afternoon in spring

i am	the horse and its bridle
i am	the post, the nail and the electric wire
i am	the creek and its banks, the bullrushes, the frog, the mallard, red-winged blackbird
i am	the hawk, black wing tips and the sky
i am	the horse, the saddle, and the woman riding, the mosquito and the dragonfly
i am	the yellow-shafted flicker
i am	the earth and the grass, the fox resting near his den (it is sunday)

afterwards, i am melancholy

(lena, a ten year old quarter horse mare, how's poco lena by here's how, and out of poco betsy sue, dun with dorsal stripe)

10/6/87

also the baseball, bat and glove. but that's for another day.

13/6/87

i have lost my voice. other things as well, but it's the voice that matters. cannot speak to tell you i love you. nothing comes when i beg you to stay.

14/6/87

a friend of mine insists he always wanted to be a preacher. there were only two problems. one, he was a heretic, and two, he could never think of anything to say.

the kind of preacher i could listen to for hours.

19/6/87

sleep brings me to a door. something is ahead of me, is coming. awake, i am afraid. it takes hours getting used to being here again.

last night was the same, and the night before.

tomorrow

2/7/87

john called, sounded so happy. says he's never slept so well, is exercising daily, feels good, is doing all the things he always wanted to.

he can't quite believe it.

7/7/87

the vase that i keep in the garden, it broke in last night's storm. flowers bruised and scattered. can you understand the depth of my sorrow? can i

7/7/87

in spring, father, seventy-four, washes his car, packs some clothes, sausage and bread, mother, they are going north. up there, land is cheap, you can still homestead. he is thinking of starting over.

14/7/87

baseball and healing. the team, the church, a common cup, the sacrament of handshake. and just when the last thing i wanted was to be healed.

16/7/87

dad visiting from ontario. breakfast at nick's inn. we talk and talk. there are things we can't agree on.

back at the apartment, i read him "childhood and russia." when i look up there is sorrow in his face. outside, jesus is weeping.

in the afternoon, the morris stampede. the cows and horses of my youth. and his.

driving home, he touches my shoulder. we've had a good day. he thinks it may be the last.

20/7/87

i believe in baseball. pitching duels and umpires. bases loaded, base on balls, stolen base, forced play. in pitch outs, pick off plays, slap bunt, sac bunt, drag bunt, fake bunt. hit and run, double play, round the horn, pop up, line drive, strikeout. i believe in curve balls, sliders, rise balls, drop balls, don't forget about your change up. good calls, bad calls, full count, safe at first, out at home, delayed steals, uniforms, coaches. sometimes i believe in home runs too, usually it depends on who gets them.

1/8/87

the season is almost over. boys' and girls' fastball teams meet for a barbecue and dance. the food is good, the music loud, the girls are young and beautiful. the novelty of dancing with a coach wears off much too soon. in the end i am left a hundred times broken-hearted.

3/8/87

weekend tournament. watched the buddha play baseball. his concentration was excellent, he went undefeated.

5/8/87

a hawk sitting on a headstone in a graveyard just off saskatchewan highway 13. the wind is from the northwest. somewhere it is raining.

7/8/87

you're still around, though neither of us is always sure why. it's easier to start than to finish, and some days that's enough.

yesterday you called, thought maybe we should stop seeing each other for a while. (i'll admit, my breath caught.) that way, you said, we could start over again later in the week.

Train Journals

May 5, 1987

9:23 a.m.

via rail station, jasper.

a beautiful sunny day, that's how vacations usually end. the train that will take us to winnipeg has just pulled in. about thirty japanese tourists get off. they gather to wander up and down the pavement. one spreads his arms, looks skyward, takes a deep breath. another takes pictures of his wife with the conductor, she must stand just so. there is one camera per couple. they must document. pictures completed, they are gone.

minutes later, i see them and their luggage beside a brewster charter bus.

9:40 a.m.

m. suggests i guess what she dreamt about last night. then before i can, tells me she dreamt she was pregnant. i tell her i dreamt about outlaws and mexico.

9:48 a.m.

there's a bench here up against the wall of the train station. a warm spot in the sun. we know the train is about to leave. still we sit, look anxiously at our watches, sit some more, our time in jasper is over too soon.

10:15 a.m.

breakfast in the dining car. i am prepared to be grouchy, unpleasant about the service. the charm of the waiter disarms me. for now.

10:30 a.m.

keep my eyes outside the window. i want to see moose or bear. have seen lots of elk, deer, big horn, canada geese, mallards, canada jay. even a couple of loons, a bush wolf.

mountains slip by.

10:42 a.m.

wish i knew the names of all the ducks we've seen.

10:45 a.m.

no moose, no bear. beaver dams, lodges. no beaver.

10:52 a.m.

m. wants to know what i'm writing, wants to read. i say no. she is irritated. probably wants attention. she begins to imitate my mannerisms.

11:12 a.m.

m. is excited. says she saw a moose. seems to enjoy the fact that it upsets me. it was probably an elk, i'm not sure she knows the difference.

11:21 a.m.

in the middle of an empty field, a crow perched on the roof of a rusted car. the train stops.

11:27 a.m.

wave at a group of linemen standing along the track. m. thinks the one on the right with the blue shirt is good looking. i question her taste in men.

11:33 a.m.

lethargy. not ready for winnipeg and work.

11:45 a.m.

a small stone monument on the south side of the track, an inscription in bronze, i think it says 1986. m. asks if we are close to hinton. is it safe to assume that disaster comes only at night?

11:59 a.m.

back in our room, m. stops at the mirror, fingers shuffle black hair. she sits beside me, the sun in her lap, hand warm on my thigh

1:30 p.m.

wake from a nap. still sunny. mountains are gone, hills forested, stands of evergreen, here and there a farm.

1:40 p.m.

village of wildwood, alberta. kids waving. m. grins, waves back. looks at me.

1:46 p.m.

i wonder why i am doing this. m. says to pass the time. do i detect sarcasm?

i wonder how many entries i need to make this work, better still, what to put in them to make it work.

1:51 p.m.

train stops, where are we? south side of the track shows signs of a village. edson? evansburg? edson should be bigger. one thing's sure, it isn't jasper. i need a map.

2:14 p.m.

m. yawns, i guess she's still sleepy.

2:25 p.m.

i think we must be nearing edmonton, suddenly a large lake i didn't know about. looks like a resort area here on the north side. a man and his wife fishing, he waves.

on the south side of the lake i see a factory, three stacks. grotesque

2:30 p.m.

harbour haven.

2:35 p.m.

m. curled up on the floor of our little room, asleep. she has taken off her mask, looks like a child again. i turn away.

2:49 p.m.

cavell.

3:00 p.m.

m. is awake.

what is it that irritates your partner most about you? the newlywed game. m. thinks we should go on, could probably win.

3:05 p.m.

farmer out on his field seeding, seeding a crop he can't afford to seed, a crop he can't afford not to seed, out on his field.

3:15 p.m.

edmonton. tracks run through the industrial part of town, ugly. still it is spring. green shows through cracks in the concrete. poplar and willow grow in the most unlikely places. red-winged blackbirds nest in little sloughs. bullrushes bent on reclamation.

3:28 p.m.

via rail station, edmonton.

m. suggests we go for a walk, this room is no longer big enough for two of us.

5:16 p.m.

walked to the edmonton art gallery, just two blocks. it was a rush tour but m. and i managed to get a good look at a collection of buddhist images.

then back to the train station where we were kept waiting for an extra half hour, couldn't even get back on the train.

in the waiting room, a young woman, about twenty, with long legs, blonde, her t shirt tight against round breasts, pointing nipples. i don't think m. noticed

now we are rolling again.

6:02 p.m.

Bruce.

outside, gently rolling prairie, farms, fields. for every puddle a pair of ducks, for every hundred bullrushes two red-winged blackbirds.

will never travel without my birdbook again.

6:15 p.m.

viking. what? here in the middle of alberta?

m. is talking to the conductor.

6:38 p.m.

inventory. three red angus, two mallards, five limousin, three meadowlarks, a sandpiper, seven or eight ducks, a dozen herefords some with calves, two crows, a freight train, four horses, no moose, two mules (don't ask me how i know), nine charolais, more ducks and blackbirds, twenty three sheep (in irma) one is obviously lost, a hawk, two canada geese, one farmer

7:04 p.m.

where are we? stopped again. freight train passing on the south. a moment ago i saw four or five helicopters. an army base? wainwright. i wonder about cruise missiles.

7:34 p.m.

ribstone, alberta.

7:40 p.m.

just past chauvin, an old grey windmill you'd expect not to be working anymore, but it is. quarter mile downwind the latest in versatile.

i tell m. about the farmall A rowcrop we used on the farm in 1959. i'm not sure she's interested. wasn't even born yet.

7:48 p.m.

artland, saskatchewan wheat pool. sometime in the last few minutes we bumped across a border, didn't feel a thing.

8:10 p.m.

shadows growing. earth turning its back to the sun. deer are coming out to feed. our train has disturbed several, others farther away simply lift their heads to watch, then continue to graze.

8:18 p.m.

m. and i not talking much. in this confined space our words pounce on each other.

8:25 p.m.

unity, saskatchewan. near the elevator i see something that looks like the cross between a tabby and a bobcat. grey coat, short tail, long hind legs, a little too big for a housecat. strange union.

8:34 p.m.

this is a tough assignment.

9:05 p.m.

in the lounge car for a drink while the porter makes our beds. m. is drinking tea. she is angry because i told the conductor we would be using both beds.

9:35 p.m.

new york is big, this is biggar. and if you're from saskatchewan you know that's an old joke, but if you're not

m. frowns, she's from saskatchewan.

by the time we get to biggar, the fields have more or less stretched themselves flat. the sky is prairie, well past sundown but not quite dark. here and there the lights of a tractor, farmers seeding under a half moon, tired but tuned to the roar of their engines and, maybe, to the last few minutes of the oilers/red wings game. their children at home, sleeping.

9:44 p.m.

in our room again. m. insists on the bottom bunk. i plead prostate problems, old age. besides, i'm not ready to go to bed yet and need some place to sit.

10:05 p.m.

getting ready for bed.

i tell m. that years ago i had a friend who was unable to go while on a train. she asks if he is still alive. i say he is, although his wife has left him and he no longer travels by train.

m. laughs. it's all right then.

10:33 p.m.

via rail station, saskatoon.

tonight i'll fall asleep in saskatoon. m. on the top bunk, i can hear her breathe, the tensions of the day have vanished.

May 6, 1987

8:56 a.m.

slept well and long, again failed to stumble on the dotted line. m. and i wake to the green of manitoba, a sky as blue as any in jasper. the train pulls steadily toward portage la prairie, winnipeg.

9:21 a.m.

breakfast in the dining car, almost as good as home. the waiter is pleasant. m. is cheerful.

10:15 a.m.

union station, winnipeg. almost home